COUNTRY LIVING

500 QUICK & EASY DECORATING PROJECTS & IDEAS

COUNTRY LIVING

500 QUICK & EASY DECORATING PROJECTS & IDEAS

From the Editors of COUNTRY LIVING Magazine

Text by Dominique DeVito

Hearst Books
A Division of Sterling Publishing Co., Inc.
New York

Copyright © 2007 by Hearst Communications, Inc.

Library of Congress Cataloging-in-Publication Data
DeVito, Dominique C.
Country living: 500 sensational quick and easy decorating projects & ideas / Dominique C. DeVito.
p. cm.
Includes index.
ISBN-13: 978-1-58816-606-7
ISBN-10: 1-58816-606-6
1. Decoration and ornament, Rustic--Handbooks, manuals, etc. 2. Interior decoration--Handbooks, manuals, etc.
I. Country living (New York, N.Y.) II. Title. III. Title: 500 sensational quick and easy decorating projects & ideas.
NK1994.R87.D48 2007
747--dc22
2006027588

10 9 8 7 6 5 4 3 2 1

Published by Hearst Books
A Division of Sterling Publishing Co., Inc.
387 Park Avenue South, New York, NY 10016

Cover and interior design by 3+Co. (www.threeandco.com)
Jacket photographs: *front cover*, Jonn Coolidge; *spine*, Keith Scott Morton; *back cover right*, David Prince; *back cover left*, Tim Street-Porter

Country Living and Hearst Books are trademarks
of Hearst Communications, Inc.

www.countryliving.com

Distributed in Canada by Sterling Publishing
c/o Canadian Manda Group, 165 Dufferin Street
Toronto, Ontario, Canada M6K 3H6

Distributed in Australia by Capricorn Link (Australia) Pty. Ltd.
P.O. Box 704, Windsor, NSW 2756 Australia

Manufactured in China

ISBN 13: 978-1-58816-606-7
ISBN 10: 1-58816-606-6

Table of Contents

Introduction

Empty rooms are as intimidating to the would-be decorator as blank pages are to the would-be writer. Filling them in ways that give meaning can seem like an endless project—or it can become a means to discover things about yourself, your family, your lifestyle, and the things you love. Gleaned from the pages of *Country Living*, the ideas in this book are designed to make the adventure—the process—of decorating less daunting and more playful and inspiring. There are tips about color choices; how to work with textures, patterns, and styles when putting rooms together; organizing collectibles; turning found objects into functional or fanciful accessories; and much, much more. With 500 tips organized by rooms, you can beautify and personalize any area of your house.

—Nancy Mernit Soriano
Editor in Chief, *Country Living*

Chapter 1   Entries and Hallways

1

The calming influence of the color green is intensified in a collection of old vases and bottles that are artfully arranged on a simple shelf.

2

Entryways that serve as mudrooms need to be durable as well as functional. Using horseshoes as hooks adds a rustic touch to a space that's designed to be well used.

3

—

Bring the attention from room to room by repeating a trim color as a main color in a nearby room, or successively changing the tint of paints in adjacent spaces. A color-coordinated primary object like this desk adds to the perspective.

4
—

Decorative trim work adds
ornamentation that enhances
the character of a home. Here,
arches and columns create a
dramatic entryway.

5

Beat the winter blahs by nurturing an amaryllis. The dramatic flower, available in many colors, takes eight to twelve weeks to bloom, making it the perfect fall-to-winter transitional plant.

6

Transportable organization meets fun and fashion when colorful totes like these rattan bags are labeled and hung on a wall covered with gingham wallpaper.

7

Old clocks that no longer tell the time make a graphic wall arrangement when hung together. Add charm by placing a rustic table—with its original finish and topped with a tin vase of daisies—under the arrangement.

8

A contrasting trim like the pale blue that's around the front door here is all that's needed to help pop your curb appeal.

9

When you know pets are going to be climbing on the furniture, incorporate pet-friendly fabrics that are durable and machine washable.

10

Fresh hydrangeas in a white ceramic vase are a summertime must and add color and personality to a hallway featuring a dark, dramatic staircase with contrasting dark and white wood.

11

A basic bench can be accessorized in all kinds of ways, the most practical of which is with accent cushions and the seat-cushion fabric itself. Open compartments below offer storage for shoes, blankets, and whatever else can fit.

12

Custom-built cubbies with space for baskets and peg rails are perfect for storing umbrellas, bags, winter wear, and other items in mudrooms and entryways.

13

A gold-framed mirror echoes
the honey-toned maple floors and
complements the warm coloring
of the "slip-proof" wool carpeting.
The mirror enlarges the space and
fills the empty wall.

14

Why buy new furniture when the next yard sale may land you a one-of-a-kind something that can make all the difference in a special spot? This cabinet's multiple panes make finding extra linens easy.

15

Customize fabric bouquets to complement your decor using remnants left over from crafting projects. A single contrasting color adds drama.

16

A seven-foot-long bench is the centerpiece of this entryway without taking up too much space. Instead of adding pillows, put flowers in old trophies used as vases on one end of the bench for a decorative touch.

17

The unique collection of wall hangings above the bench reflects the family's love of history and nature. The eclecticism of the selections is balanced by the color theme and by the stenciled backdrop.

18

A strong but soothing color in an entryway sets the mood for the whole house. Here, architectural details are painted white to create a sophisticated and welcoming foyer.

19

Quilts can be welcoming works of art when hung on large walls. Too pretty to stash away, they can also find their way onto balustrades, where they are especially complementary to wide-planked wood floors.

20

An eclectic collection of glass bottles can be displayed in rows according to size (or randomly) along window sills or stairway ledges.

21

For dog lovers, there's nothing like cast-iron doorstops resembling their favorite breeds to add whimsy and personality to a room.

22

Reflecting the light from the double front doors is the job of the multiple mirrors positioned along the stairwell.

23

A rich, saturated color makes an excellent foil to cherry-stained and white-painted wood. Hang a throw on the end of a banister for easy access on chilly evenings.

24

Throw something modern into the mix to shake things up. A white star light fixture does the job here, while unifying the passageway with the next room.

25

A rustic bench provides a spot for further organizing miscellaneous items that are left in entryways, such as antique quilts and an oversized picnic basket.

26

The gentle curves of this small wooden table and chair soften the rigid corner of the entryway where they have been placed.

27

A large bouquet of fresh and fragrant flowers in an entryway guarantees a cheerful and memorable greeting for everyone who enters the house.

28

Simplicity and style distinguish this cheery entrance. The green-themed bouquets pick up on the wall color, and a convenient stepping stool can be stored away under the decorative table.

29

Painting a wall a color that's reminiscent of new spring growth, showy summer shades, the luster of fall green apples, and the promise of greenery brings the outdoors in all year long.

30

Resist updating the imperfections of an old home. This well-used stair banister is original to the house and is part of its charm.

31

Express your creative color sense in an entry- or hallway with a chair painted a luscious shade of pink and finished with an espresso-colored seat.

32

Going bold with color works when the wood trim throughout the house is painted a high-gloss white, as it helps the colors pop. The intensity of the colors should be equal, and their hues should be incorporated from room to room.

33

The earth tones and white trim help pull the mango color from one room to the next, and draw the eye through this series of adjoining rooms.

34

An old milk jug painted a vibrant color by the front door in a foyer serves as a distinctive and practical repository for walking canes or umbrellas.

35

A floor that is functional yet fun
is achieved in a small entryway by
pairing checkerboard-patterned
tiles and a bold throw rug.

36

A mirror in an entryway helps guests transition from outside to inside and can instantly make a small space seem larger.

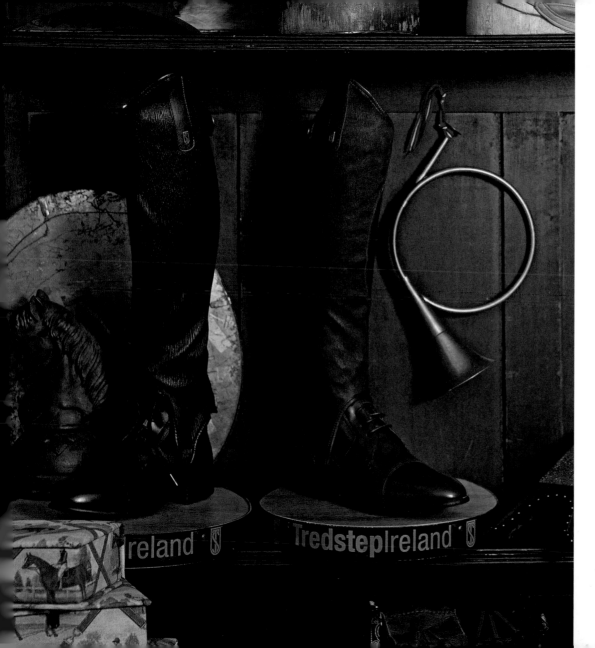

37

If your passions are horses and riding, you can turn a collection of helmets, boots, and gloves into a display by arranging them with equine-themed art.

38

Red steps located right inside the front door pop against walls and trim painted stark white, and offer a warm welcome and a colorful passageway.

39

Create a bold, dramatic entryway with an eclectic mix of flea market and antique store finds, such as this character-filled cabinet and tarnished mirror.

40

Show off your collection of crafts where you think they will look best. These horses made of fabric scraps are right at home on a tweed-covered settee.

41

If you have the space—and the desire—you may want to consider having a mural painted in part of your house.

42

The large painted diamond pattern on the floor is reminiscent of a style popular in the mid-1800s and adds charm to this upstairs hallway.

Chapter 2 Kitchens

43

Foster a country look in the
kitchen with simple elements
like distinctive woodwork
(here, unpainted pine) and
marble counters.

44

Recessed shelving is a handy spot for displaying useful and visually appealing collectibles like creamers, pitchers, and dry-goods containers.

45

Get organized and add color and texture to the kitchen by storing cookware in baskets, like these wicker ones that complement the neutral earth tones around them.

46

Awaken an overlooked wall with
a series of framed prints hung
one over another on the thin wall
space between two windows.

47

When you love something, let it out. If red is your color, find places for it, in all its variations, in the rooms you like to spend the most time in, like the kitchen.

48

Position colors and patterns so that your eyes travel around them. Here, the patterns on the bowls are slightly mirrored in the clock, and a small plate with similar colors keeps the composition from being static.

49

Clean lines, contrasting colors, and uncluttered surfaces give this kitchen a refreshing, inviting, and easy-to-live-in feel.

50

If you're looking to spruce up your kitchen, a couple of quick fixes that won't break the bank are finding new hardware for the cabinets and installing a new faucet for the sink.

51

Blue-and-white transferware arranged symmetrically in the corner of a breakfast nook stands out against cream-colored walls and picks up the blue in the fabric used on the seat covers and bench.

52

Pink appliances are the showpieces in this kitchen, where simple white cabinetry and a checkered linoleum floor offset the rosy hues and create a retro, cheery atmosphere.

53

Working with a common color theme, arrange plates of different sizes and patterns in descending order by size for a pretty focal point over a small table in the dining area of a kitchen.

54

White, vertically oriented tiles extending all the way up to a stainless steel range hood will bring a feeling of greater height to a kitchen.

55

One way to vary the walls is to use colored grout with white tiles. In this cozy country kitchen, a chocolate-colored grout creates a gingham effect.

56

Place a long narrow table in a
kitchen with no defined eating
nook. It puts diners in the middle
of things and can serve as extra
prep space in a pinch.

57

To house a large collection of cookbooks and keep them handy in the kitchen, construct custom shelves on either side of and above the refrigerator.

58

An antique dish rack makes a unique display piece while keeping pieces handy for use. Shelves below offer space for bowls and an eclectic collection of teapots and creamers.

59

A recessed area of the kitchen is painted a slightly warmer tone for visual interest and to further differentiate it from the rest of the room.

60

A kitchen chandelier becomes whimsical—and even practical— by hanging mismatched porcelain teacups from its branches.

61

Instead of an island, place a moveable, low-to-the-ground table in the middle of a kitchen to create a kid-friendly eating area.

62

A large armoire with shelves, hooks, and vertical compartments can be stocked with everything from pots and pans to cookbooks, trays, and utensils.

63

Cupboards are excellent showcases for kitchenware, plus arrangements of photographs and personal treasures. Leave the doors open for easy access and a decorative display.

64

Make the most of small spaces by using furniture that folds away. These chairs are transformed into art when put on display, especially when painted a bright color.

65

A simple wooden table can be painted a neutral color, such as white, and embellished with a stripe or a stenciled pattern around the outside.

66

The beauty and durability of a large pine table in the kitchen is paired with a practical stainless-steel top. The vintage porcelain sink and mismatched stools add to the charm of the room.

67

A top shelf provides additional storage and opportunity for displaying a collection—in this case, glasses. A towel rack below is convenient while drying dishes.

68

A plain table and pair of wingback chairs under a pendant lamp create a cozy nook in the kitchen for enjoying coffee or doing homework.

69

Just as no two guests are alike, your kitchen-table chairs needn't be, either. Mix and match to add comfort, informality, and individual style to your seating.

70

Help usher summer in by growing small pots of herbs in a sunny kitchen window in early spring. When the ground thaws, transplant your little garden outdoors.

71

The freestanding pie stand was once a staple of French country cooks. Today, it's being recast as a handsome decorative feature that can display a host of items.

72

Unaligned restaurant supply shelves keep canisters, teapots, teacups, and various kitchen accessories within easy reach while making the wall more interesting visually.

73

A distressed mantel hung in front of a kitchen window makes a unique shelf upon which to display vintage coffee servers, flowers, herbs, and other collectibles.

74

Sheer linens can be hemmed with fabric glue and secured with curtain pin hooks to hang from a rod over a window.

75

The tiling that serves as a short backsplash along the cabinetry near the sink is extended onto the adjoining wall to enhance its appearance and add texture.

76

Shelves of natural planks reflect the warm earth tones of the rest of the space while showing off a collection of white porcelain china.

77

The new stainless-steel dishwasher and range merge into the overall scheme of this kitchen, with its zinc-wrapped countertops.

78

Line the back of a kitchen eating area cabinet with vintage fabric or wallpaper to help a favorite collection stand out.

79

A witty way of introducing color
is to put a white-based gingham
check on the ceiling. This makes
the color appear lighter than a
solid hue.

80

For a festive and inspiring focal
point, try a multihued backsplash
that incorporates the color theme
of the kitchen.

81

High-gloss acrylic applied to
butcher block seals the wood,
brings out its warmth, and
helps the kitchen shine.

82

Here, the black backsplash and countertops are reflected in the checkerboard pattern on the floor. The mustard-colored walls bring out the white cabinets.

83

A round table promotes harmony and helps conversation flow over breakfast or lunch in the kitchen.

84

Enamel canisters can be arranged on a kitchen counter so short ones intermingle with tall ones for a less structured, more playful look.

85

Window-paned cabinets are a means of introducing more color to a kitchen. In this case, they showcase dinnerware and stemware in shades of green that are picked up in other pieces in the room.

86

A trio of shiny white pitchers employed as vases make lovely containers for cut or planted white tulips and create a fresh, springlike atmosphere in a charming country kitchen.

87

Mount hooks in a cabinet with glass doors to make the most of the space and create an eclectic display.

88

Once a theme is established—like green-hued glassware—finding additional pieces of it to display becomes a hobby that pays off in completing a look.

89

An antique Magic Chef 1000 Series oven from the 1930s is the stunning centerpiece of this retro-style kitchen.

90

What's more cheerful than a kitchen with candy-colored accents, including the table and chairs? All it takes is perseverance in shopping flea markets for the table and chairs, and the selection of paint colors to work with the rest of the room.

91

A painted floor can hide the faults of an otherwise dreary wood finish. To redo it, decide on a design; sand then prime the entire floor with the lighter color; draw the pattern on with water-soluble colored pencils and a ruler; apply the color; and finish with a sealant.

92

Clean lines and sleek, minimalist appliances dominate in this open and airy space, providing a sense of greater expansion.

93

In a pale-hued space, the addition of a few large, colorful items—like a vase filled with lemons and a vintage sign behind the stove—adds vitality.

94

An island with plenty of leg room and a cast of stools and chairs help bring people in to chat and share the day.

95

In this kitchen, the countertops are crafted of different materials to suit the work that's done there: marble for the cooking zone, stainless steel around the sink, and oiled walnut for the center island.

96

Simple, open shelves adorned with vintage brackets become a functional focal point in a kitchen, and provide extra storage space.

97

In a kitchen, a simple metal bakery rack is the perfect place to display a colorful, eclectic collection of kitchenware piled high.

98

Two ways to add more space and convenience to a small kitchen: Install a countertop at the end of the room to create an eating area and prep zone, and put up a rack that has both a shelf and hooks for hanging pots.

99

A quirky set of prints can be mounted in fairly inexpensive frames and hung together to create an instant collection and point of interest.

100

Here, a panel of the basement door has been covered with chalkboard paint to give this small kitchen a big memo board to write on.

101

A bench with storage extends the seating area and provides a place to store bulk items like paper towels or bottled water.

102

Give a simple space an updated look with chrome-faced appliances and simple hardware for drawers and cabinets.

103

Break up a monochromatic palette and add comfort in a kitchen with a multicolored runner in front of the sink/stove/dishwasher area of the room.

104

Turn what might be a cramped and inefficient space at the end of a small kitchen into a delightful breakfast nook. Bring in elements that work together and make the best use of the space with a round table, seating bench with storage, and clean colors that open the space.

105

Modern stainless-steel appliances are given a furniture treatment in this rustic kitchen with planked walls and a beamed ceiling.

106

Warm, tan-colored walls unite the various shades of wood in this country kitchen. A unique touch is the frieze of dried maple leaves alternating with yellowed pages from a child's workbook above the cabinet.

107

The microwave has its own "house" on the wall, making it a handy but decorative feature.

108

The arched cherry-wood cupboard is both a place to stash everyday items and a display piece for collectibles.

109

A handcrafted island helps bring
a woodsy feel to the kitchen,
as do the faux vines circling the
droplights overhead.

110

To vary the look of storage areas,
some cabinets are open, some
are screened pie safe–style, while
others have beadboard doors.

111

Consider hanging a small ladder from the ceiling to function as a pot rack. Make sure the wood is sturdy enough to support the hardware and the cookware.

112

The rich, bold red of this shelving makes the collection of McCoy and Hall pottery it supports really stand out. Your current collections can tell you a lot about what colors you're drawn to. Use that knowledge to choose other colors when expanding the collection.

113

An informal dining area in a large kitchen is decorated in a primary color scheme, picking up strong blues, yellows, and reds. The tablecloth brings everything together.

114

Beadboard used as a kitchen backsplash adds a nice textural element in a cottage-style kitchen with white appliances and window shutters.

115

Vinyl tiles in the same color family as the cabinets and backsplash form a checkerboard on the kitchen floor and make for easy cleanup.

116

Pale blue walls are accented by pure white cupboards and trim. Open stainless-steel shelves complement the range and countertops.

117

Small tiles accentuate the mosaic pattern behind kitchen counters and make an interesting backsplash and visual point.

Chapter 3 Bathrooms

118

With some fresh herbs from a farmers' market, create a personal bouquet for the bath that will perk up and refresh you or a guest after a long, hot summer day.

119

Spruce up a metal dresser with a rust remover and paint to transform even inexpensive retro office or medical furniture into a showy and practical piece.

120

Traditional tile or beadboard was replaced with white-painted pressed tin to give a unique look to—and dress up—these bathroom walls.

121

An old wooden mantel installed next to a clawfoot tub serves as an elegant and convenient shelf for bath salts, candles, flowers, and other bath luxuries.

122

A skylight brings additional light and cheer to a small bathroom where a tiled shower provides refuge from the stresses of the day.

123

A chair can be used for all kinds of things in a bathroom. The slipcover should be a fabric that can be washed if lotion or bath oil is spilled on it.

124

If your space is big enough, consider the ultimate luxury of twin pedestal sinks in a master or guest bathroom.

125

Pouches of linen tied with delicate ribbons make pretty sachets for bath salts or potpourri ready for display in a guest bathroom.

126

An armoire can make up for the
lack of a closet in any room. In a
humid bathroom, one that is
fronted with chicken wire allows
air to circulate and attractive
accessories to be displayed.

127

For the ultimate entertainment indulgence, this master bathroom mirror incorporates an LCD screen that's invisible unless the television is on.

128

For a bathroom imbued with country charm, consider floor-to-ceiling beadboard.

129

A circular shower rod gives just enough privacy in a freestanding tub, and you can experiment with different shower curtains to give the room the right feel.

130

Don't feel like you have to hide your bathroom supplies. Here towels are stored in open shelves under the sink.

131

A plain butcher-block sideboard is transformed with decorative trim and a collection of seashells glued to the drawer. A starfish becomes the drawer pull.

132

For small spaces, multifunctional pieces are key. This chrome-and-glass medical table in the bathroom has also seen use in other rooms as a bar for entertaining.

133

Tile extended up a wall and around a tub gives an almost sunken-tub feeling. Vary the tile pattern around the top and include a border for extra appeal.

134

Shells belong near water, so what better place for them than in the bathroom? This shell border was created by gluing the shells in place. The theme is extended to the chandelier over the tub.

135

Your vintage tub isn't complete without a shower curtain made from a chenille bedspread. First, hem to the correct length, then install grommets to hold the shower hooks.

136

Silver and cut crystal are timeless accessories and, in the bathroom, can be displayed in groupings, either empty or filled with toiletries such as swabs, cotton balls, and eau de toilette.

137

A vanity that is draped in silk
resembles a skirt's bustle and is
romantic to its core. Hang balloon
shades from the window above
for an even more decadent look.

138

Flea-market finds are the staple of this high-energy bathroom. A cerulean dresser desk has been transformed into a vanity, and a resin ceiling medallion has been made into the mirror.

139

Make a new wall look old by
smearing spackling here and there,
spreading it, and then painting on
washes of browns in the same
palette, from soft creams to
deeper hues.

140

Linen is classic and versatile, and wears well for life's everyday items like hand towels, tablecloths, and upholstery used for seat cushions.

141

Translucent blue tile in an oversized shower is inviting and refreshing, and gives a watery effect that's perfect for the bathroom.

142

Cultivate a soothing atmosphere in the bathroom with simple lines, minimal accessories, and the peaceful yet cheery combination of white and pale yellow.

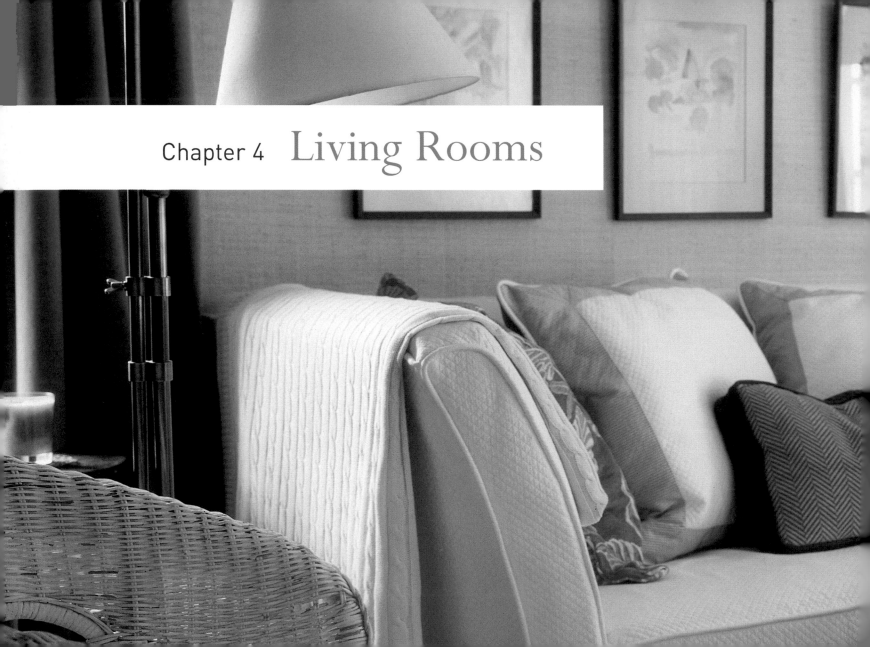

Chapter 4　Living Rooms

143

There's nothing like a fireplace to add warmth and hominess, and with gas and electric fireplaces providing almost carefree alternatives to burning wood, any home can be outfitted with one. The style options are plentiful as well.

144

Add visual interest to a plain painted wall with an application of a lighter or darker complementary shade applied through a stencil. You can even design your own stencils for a truly personal touch.

145

Tweed, plaid, velvet, and leather give this neutral scheme interest and vitality. Closely placed mismatched chairs add to the sense of coziness and comfort of this living room.

146

Details—such as piping that contrasts with the primary color scheme of window treatments while picking up other colors in the room—can complete the picture.

147

The flat-screen-television-as-art idea works here above a classically appointed mantel. The television is out of the way and is not the focal point of the room.

148

One distinctive fabric can set the design tone of an entire room. Here, the silhouette print on the curtains is carried over to the framed silhouettes on the mantelpiece.

149

Oil painting portraits found at antique shows and estate sales instill a sense of history, especially when placed in a room filled with other antiques, such as the daybed shown here.

150

A filled bookcase can support a decoratively framed painting, which can be moved or changed to create different moods.

151

Frequent visits by two- and four-legged guests are accommodated with a durable carpet of sea grass. Fringes around the leather sofas can conceal shy cats and prevent scuff marks from the heels of children's shoes.

152

Slightly distressed leather club chairs are at once traditional and contemporary—and extremely comfortable.

153

The open shelves of an étagère display objects of differing sizes without taking up too much wall space.

154

There are many ways to divide a space. Here, a rescued piece of gingerbread railing has become an informal room divider.

155

The pale palette and gently worn furniture in this cozy but open living and dining area are accented with pieces whose dark edges lend drama.

156

Group items by color and shape for a classic look. Open shelves on either side of a double window in a living room provide ample space for displaying assorted collections—of trophies, vases, or candlesticks.

157

An old mantel is personalized with a handmade mosaic fashioned from broken teacups—making it truly a one-of-a-kind.

158

Mirrors break up a space and add light and visual appeal when placed against each other on top of a fireplace in a living room.

159

A simple earthenware jar is spruced up by an encircling dainty wreath of pine boughs and winter grasses, and is the perfect receptacle for a sprig of dried flowers.

160

A table and two chairs in front of a fireplace offer the perfect spot for enjoying a cup of tea or playing a game by the fire on chilly evenings.

161

Using period-appropriate stencils to create a simple yet elegant focal point above a fireplace mantle gives a living room style, authenticity, and a personal touch.

162

Bandboxes—popular as lightweight storage containers in the 18th and 19th centuries—make beautiful decorative storage units today, especially when paired with other antiques, such as books.

163

Establish a focal point with a single dramatic element in a living room, for example a tight grid of similarly themed prints flanked by matching urns.

164

Leaded-glass doors are used to extend the open look of the fireplace on either side of an expansive mantel.

165

Urns used as vases on a mantle or coffee table can complement a classic look and come in a variety of shapes, styles, and colors.

166

Silk window treatments pulled to one side allow for a touch of flounce in an otherwise demure room.

167

The impact of floor-to-ceiling windows is maximized with leggy furniture that allows light in from every direction. A touch of a mustard color in the room makes it even brighter.

168

When preparing for a party, dress up a modest ice bucket by perching it on a stool or plant stand and encircling it in the greenery of your choice.

169

The overall style of this cottage living room is designed to be an extension of what's outside—to play on color and light. The crisp cotton piqué slipcover showcases a host of blue- and green-themed pillows.

170

Grass cloth on the walls reflects the outdoor light and gives the room an organic, living, breathing quality.

171

A refurbished and truncated set of stairs makes a multi-leveled side table for easy access to an assortment of books and other accessories.

172

Let a collection of paintings set the tone of a living room, as the dramatic display of floral still lifes that hang in this room.

173

For a rich, homey feel, go with a brown palette and lots of texture. With brown it's easy to mix tweed with knit and wool; a wicker basket filled with rolled yarn contributes nuances of color and texture.

174

Yellow walls and ceiling capture sunlight from the wall of French doors, infusing the room with summer all year long.

175

Plenty of upholstered furniture in a large room keeps it cozy. Choose variety of pieces to give the room personality.

176

Dominant patterns can peacefully coexist when they're grounded, as they are here by the geometric grid in the rug and the floral motif throughout.

177

This homeowner went bold with a paint that matches an antique variety of fruit growing in her orchard, some samples of which are collected in a white bowl on the table.

178

A collection of stepstools—all different sizes and colors—forms the basis for an arrangement of books and other curios in built-in bookcases.

179

When a room is color-coordinated, all sorts of accessories will work in it, such as the eclectic shell mirror-and-candleholders on the far wall and shell-encrusted lamp on the near table.

180

Transform an armoire by painting it a soft shade of pink with white trim, and finishing the back with pink-accented wallpaper. It's the perfect showcase for all of your prettiest pink things.

181

Resist the urge to refinish or paint imperfect antique pieces—such as the coffee table, chairs, and chest shown here. Combining new and old furniture in a living room creates a homey, lived-in feel.

182

A neutral-patterned rug brings the entire room together, while a pink area shag rug unifies the seating space and adds some pizzazz.

183

A jumble of patterns could disturb the balance in this room, so pillows and throws have been carefully selected. The pink throws match the area rug, and the pillows pick up the color in the drapes.

184

Pink can be both a restful and exciting color. To keep it from overwhelming a space, balance it with plenty of white. The sofa and matching chairs, plus the white walls and trim, keep this room quiet so its pink accents can pop.

185

The formality of this room is established with dark walls and classic white trim. Red accents and a variety of fabrics used provide plenty of dramatic counterpoints throughout.

186

A sole distinctive chair covered in a fabric that echoes the palette of the rest of the room is a lovely conversation piece and is perfectly situated in a corner of the room.

187

A customized mirror replaces wood paneling in an alcove, helping enlarge the room. Short on wall space? Lean framed photographs or paintings against a wall or mirror, atop a shelf or mantle.

188

Cathedral ceilings are balanced with floor-to-ceiling bookcases, whose shelves can also be used to showcase artwork and other collectibles and knick-knacks.

189

Stone urns, more commonly found in outdoor formal gardens, bring a touch of formality and the outdoors inside when "potted" with artificial ivy.

190

The recessed spaces in this cabinet are painted a bright yellow to tie in with the other yellow touches in the room.

191

The sofa, chairs, and ottomans share a mustard and chocolate palette, though they are all upholstered differently.

192

To pull off an historical look in a Colonial house, work with simple antique pieces like iron candleholders and a basic rocker by an enormous fireplace.

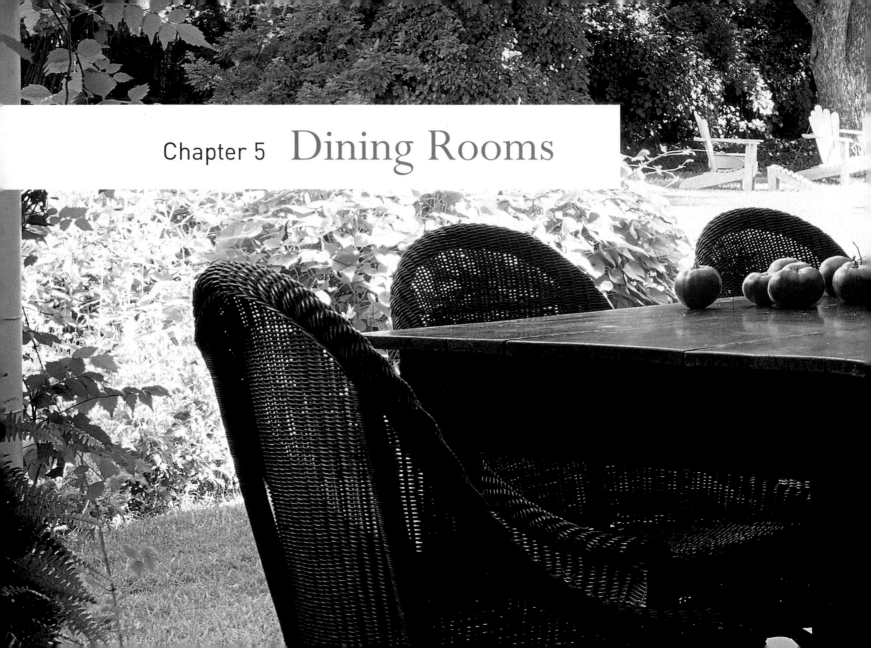

Chapter 5 Dining Rooms

193

Toile wallpaper applied inside a cupboard provides visual appeal to a cabinet corner while helping to showcase the sparsely displayed collectibles inside it.

194

For a cool, dramatic, and chic look, accent a mostly white room with black-and-white-patterned upholstered dining room chairs, pillows, and other bold accessories.

195

Wood, wood everywhere: A collection of wooden bowls is supported on open shelving so that their colors can complement and contrast with those of the wall and floor.

196

Historically accurate paints set this space apart and add authenticity. If that's a direction you want to go, research the period and what your options are.

197

An easy, elegant, and accessible way of storing silverware is to put it—sorted by type—in vintage silver cups arranged on a silver platter.

198

Once you have a color scheme chosen, you can mix and match the patterns and shapes of your tableware for memorable settings. Match floral arrangements to the dishes.

199

A variety of textures defines this dining room, from the dramatic floor-length draperies to the Aubusson rug to the fanciful crystal chandelier that adds sparkle.

200

Slipcovers can transform dining room chairs—for a season or longer—while still allowing the beauty of the chairs to come through. Let them set the mood of the room.

201

One way to marry antique and contemporary styles in a dining room is to mount several vintage wine labels in handsome modern frames.

202

An oh-so-pale blue keeps a predominantly white dining room cool while adding a touch of contrast and color.

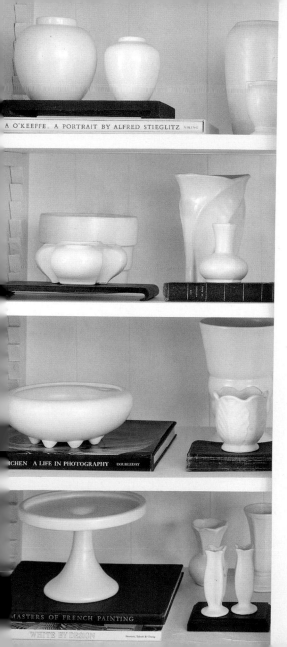

A O'KEEFFE A PORTRAIT BY ALFRED STIEGLITZ VIKING

PRIVATE PARIS

ICHEN A LIFE IN PHOTOGRAPHY DOUBLEDAY

MASTERS OF FRENCH PAINTING

WHITE BY DESIGN

HOME SIMPLE

203

The monochromatic effect of displaying white pottery on white shelves is made more visually interesting by the addition of brown trays and books to support them.

204

Turn an antique silver trophy into a handsome lamp and top it with a modern, sleek black shade to bring style and elegance to a table.

205

A hooked rug can make an eye-catching wall hanging over an antique sideboard displaying a trio of vases.

206

What better way to relax and entertain than around a 12-foot-long farmhouse table with wicker chairs? For special occasions, pull the table and chairs out onto a covered portico with a lovely garden view.

207

Linen tea towels can make attractive and absorbant oversized napkins while adding character to a table setting for intimate gatherings.

208

Pairing gold-rimmed china with a plate featuring a vibrant green floral graphic gives an effect that's classic, fun, and completely up to date for your next gathering.

209

Unique napkin rings can be made from rhinestone-studded belt buckles—found in vintage shops, flea markets, or antique stores— threaded with ribbon.

210

Miniature watering cans filled with flowers make a spring table especially inviting when used as placecards that guests can take home with them.

211

The wonderful feeling of dining alfresco in the summer can be recreated "indoors" (under a canopy) with fresh flowers on the table, floral prints, and lantern light.

212

For a sophisticated look, place a few dark elements against a mostly white color scheme; use strong, simple shapes; and go for greater impact with a few large accessories rather than many small ones.

213

For a romantic look, think curves, textures, and patterns, as shown here with the variety of curvy ceramics, slipcovered chairs, a fringed tablecloth, and hints of pale green and rose in the fruits and floral dishware.

214

A wide natural-stone fireplace takes center stage in the large living and dining area of a cabin with a rustic yet comfortable and pampered feel.

215

Overstuffed armchairs flank the
fireplace and give way to a dining
area where chairs fashioned
from branches and finished with
plaid seat cushions complete
the cozy feel.

216

Reclaimed bricks from an old factory were used for this floor to bring a sense of history to a new home.

217

A brick-red corner cupboard blends perfectly with the color scheme and serves as valuable storage space.

218

To further infuse the space with regional history and charm, wooden decoys and old baskets have been placed on the beams that support the roof.

219

A wide-planked wooden table says country; the rust-colored trim and blue-gray ceiling give an historical feel to this simple yet dramatic dining room.

220

Unique sterling serving pieces like
this fish server (called a "slice")
can make a dinner table elegant
in an instant, and can be used at
informal gatherings, as well.

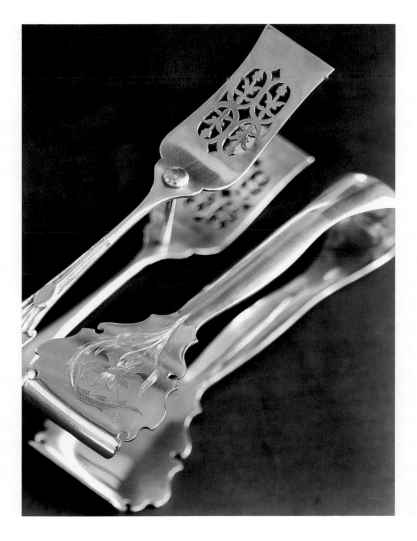

221

Decorative and fanciful sterling tongs come in a variety of sizes that allow for serving everything from asparagus to cherry tomatoes and can help grasp sugar cubes for tea or coffee.

222

Sleek and modern stemmed votives will brighten and beautify a dining table, creating just the right romantic or festive mood while preventing messy wax drips.

223

Using different sterling napkin rings is like having individual sculptures at every place setting and will surely be a topic of conversation during dinner.

224

Add an antique touch to your dining room table by using a collection of mismatched engraved silver napkin rings.

225

For a simple, summery floral arrangement, use the same color and style of candle in different sizes, then tuck freshly clipped flowers from your garden around their bases.

226

Make a dining room more dramatic and memorable by choosing a painting that incorporates the room's color scheme in a way that is big and bold and that creates a sense of balance.

227

Matching napkins with beautifully delicate roses stitched into the corners are the perfect addition to a lovely springtime table setting.

228

Setting a distinctive table is easy when you establish a strong central feature—such as color—to set the tone, letting everything else follow its lead.

229

Create a playful mood by making fanciful place settings—each charming and unique—from any ribbon, buttons, or old note cards you have stashed away.

230

Allow a color palette to capture your imagination and transform a room. Mismatched glass candlesticks with cream-colored candles work beautifully with white gold-rimmed teacups.

231

A winter dining table is graced with tiny paperwhites artfully and delicately arranged in white ceramic salt dishes for a beautiful, decorative touch.

232

Set an unusual table to entertain your guests using a collection of silver spoons engraved with different names, found in vintage and antique stores.

233

A collection of stick spatter bowls or dishes deserves to be shown off, as they are hard to find and wonderful to look at. Every piece is hand painted, the work of English and Scottish craftsmen from the 1830s to the early 20th century.

234

The colors in a painting of Provence inspired those in this warm dining room: a lemony yellow and the subtle variations of fine wood.

235

An easy-to-care-for sisal rug complements the carefree look and keeps the original, wide-planked floors from being scratched.

236

The large painting in this dining room is left unframed so it has a less formal feel. It offers a gorgeous view much like that of through a window.

237

This table "glows" with various yellows and creams, from the dinnerware to the candles and the flowers—even the label on the wine bottle.

238

Colorful toile curtains are formal enough for the dining room, yet sunny and cheery enough for the kitchen, and serve to harmonize the two rooms.

239

The intensity of the blue walls and cupboard interior in this room was achieved by applying two coats of royal blue and one of black. The color is picked up on the seat cushions and in the china on display.

240

White trim brings out the richness of the royal-blue walls; faux marble baseboards add a modern touch of distinction.

241

An old oil lamp serves as a
chandelier to cast a soft glow
over an outdoor table so that
intimate meals can linger from
the evening well into the night.

242

To add a romantic atmosphere to alfresco dining, a small collection of tapers in mismatched silver candlesticks is placed on a side buffet table.

243

Crystal, silver, votive candles, a crisp white tablecloth, and blue transferware combine for a traditional, formal table setting.

244

Fall's bounty makes a lovely arrangement on a dining room sideboard. The shapes and colors of gourds, apples, pears, and berries are accented with sprigs of greenery.

245

Warm colors like yellow, green, and red help set an active and stimulating mood, but can also cultivate feelings of welcome, intimacy, and coziness in a dining area.

246

You'll always find a spot for something special, so don't think your next captivating flea market find won't work in your house. This hot-air-balloon chandelier is a whimsical touch in an otherwise stately room.

247

Let each chair be unique, yet compatible, by mixing bold, colorful fabric patterns front to back on the same chair.

248

A 19th-century carved trencher filled with green apples makes a casual centerpiece for an antique—or any style—dining room table.

249

Don't be afraid to stray from the traditional. A vintage file cabinet can be used as a buffet with ample storage space.

250

Delight guests at a springtime luncheon with tiny, preseeded clay pots that serve as both place cards and party favors that can be taken home and enjoyed once the flowers bloom.

251

The candle chandelier is a local antiques find and is a bold focus for the room. The light cast by the candles creates a very intimate, romantic atmosphere.

252

The blue finish on top of the round white-weathered pedestal table is a unique touch that helps bring a sense of unity to the room.

253

Chairs are slipcovered in a waffle weave that's versatile enough to use indoors or take outside for alfresco dining in warm weather.

254

A collection of decorative silver platters in groups of three frame the French doors that lead to the sunporch.

255

Finishing touches help complete
and define a room. Here, lighting
in the cupboard brings attention
to the collection of spoons and tea
sets, while antique prints and
paintings fill the walls.

256

Visit your local florist to find a few unusual items to mix with things you may have growing in your garden. The personalized centerpieces you create will add color, warmth, and charm.

257

Oyster shells make great salt and pepper dishes, especially for meals enjoyed outdoors in the summertime. Before using, boil the shells to ensure they're sanitary.

258

Silver-plated pieces once used in hotels are collector's items when they have the hotel's name engraved on them; even if they don't, silver pieces always look good displayed together.

259

Add kitsch to a modern dining room with a large unframed photograph, a mismatched set of chairs, and other eclectic artwork.

260

With the appliqué options available in craft stores today, monogramming all kinds of things—including chandelier shades—is now possible ... and easy.

261

Vintage frames discovered at flea markets can be painted and hung on their own or used to frame "floating art."

262

Transferware that's too fragile to use for serving food can be turned into art, as has been done in these matching compositions.

263

A keepsake—here, a menu from a favorite restaurant—can be framed and given a place of pride on a wall or shelf.

264

Mixing old and new items—
a basket, a candelabrum, vases,
a creamer—creates a standout
effect.

265

Repurpose a dark sideboard
by painting it a color of your
choosing that will work with
the rest of your room.

266

Accessorizing a table is the most fun part. Here, a tiny glass vase at each place setting welcomes guests with three delicate tulips and a card featuring the guest's first initial.

267

Bring joy to a spring table with
this simple arrangement: Fill a
medium-size bowl with damp
moss and arrange the flowers
around the outside of the bowl.
Add a smaller bowl full of
speckled candy eggs, sugared
almonds, or pastel malt balls in
the middle, and arrange the moss
and flowers so the rim is hidden.

268

Gilded chairs are dressed up with tasseled, buttoned "ball-gown" slipcovers in a shade that nearly matches the table.

269

Silver candelabra full of white tapers are timeless, as are the small vases of daisies that will bring cheer to guests dining at each place.

270

Dress up and contemporize a dining alcove by putting bright slipcovers over the chairs and using leftover material to make placemats. Individual tumblers of flowers perfect the presentation.

271

A plain dining table and white slipcovered chairs are made more dramatic with a powerful arrangement like hydrangeas in large copper vases.

Chapter 6 Family and Great Rooms

272

Spruce up your sitting areas with pillows fashioned from hand-printed silks and linens in a variety of shapes and patterns, and with fringes and other adornments.

273

Touches of bold color can unify a room and a house, and create drama—as red does here in the throw, tablecloth, and fresh flowers in this mostly white room.

274

The muted sage-and-tan palette of this great room is accented by touches of red in the leather armchairs, pillows, wall decorations, and other accessories and knick-knacks.

275

Try replacing a traditional wood coffee table with a solid leather ottoman to add a touch of masculinity to a den or family room that is otherwise subtly feminine.

276

A single, large-scale piece like this armoire meets multiple storage needs while providing a clean, streamlined look and hiding a television, stereo, and other electronic equipment.

277

A perfectly fluted, small white vase is an elegant container for a collection of white marble eggs that would add beauty to a side table, mantle, or coffee table.

278

Breathe new life into a room and keep things simple by wallpapering just one small wall and adding complementary, patterned tablecloth—covered with a smaller, white tablecloth—to a buffet table.

279

Combining antique, vintage, and modern furnishings, unique accents, and playful surprises makes a room pop.

280

Use an antique cabinet with a
space-saving foldaway desktop
in a small den for versatility
and to avoid clutter.

281

Earthy shades of green and brown set the tone for relaxation and meditation in this quiet nook that provides a desk for sketching, painting, or other work, and an overstuffed chair for relaxing with a book.

282

Old linen tea towels can be made into soft and ultracomfortable pillowcases. Wrap a modern-looking bow around one for a contrast that works.

283

Color and eclecticism will bring any potentially hidden corner into full view. Top an antique cupboard with a tightly arranged grouping of colorful vases, urns, and other collectibles.

284

Hand-carved Bible boxes hearken back to a time when few houses had doors that locked. One's most valuable possessions were secured in individual boxes with locks.

285

A wooden bowl full of rag balls for making rugs creates a colorful centerpiece when paired with a small vase of fresh flowers on a coffee table, side table, or buffet.

286

History is embodied in this arrangement of an old oil painting hanging above a 19th-century jelly cupboard displaying an antique wooden bowl and wedding-band hogscraper candlesticks.

287

A slipcover can be a way to add texture to a room. The pillows and other pieces in the room share the mix-and-match theme— even the wicker basket is covered in fabric.

288

A stone wall is left white while the flat wall is painted a robin's egg blue to play up the qualities of texture and color.

289

A vintage mantel and repurposed iron grate give character to an otherwise plain fireplace.

290

Wood (in the side table, chest, and dishrack), clay (in the sculpture and flowerpot), and fabric (the slipcovers of the chairs) all speak to a country rusticity and simplicity that unify this corner of a family room.

291

The fringed slipcovers on the sofa, pillows, and ottoman give a comfortable and relaxed feeling to an otherwise streamlined room. Handcrafted arrangements of framed, dried flowers reflect the tone of the room.

292

A chandelier's long cord is dressed in a fabric sleeve that is complementary to the rest of the room, and its lampshades are fringed, softening the piece to seamlessly fit into the room.

293

Making a room comfortable means providing inviting places to sit, like benches with thick pads and lots of pillows, and overstuffed chairs and ottomans.

294

A sunny vase of fiery dahlias is a sight for sore eyes and will brighten any room where it is placed.

295

A 19th-century linen press hides rainy-day diversions including a television, a movie library, CDs, and board games in this bright, open, yet comfortable family room.

296

Black-and-white prints in dark frames help ground a white and cream–paletted room that's further defined by the textures of the fabrics and the slats in the wall.

297

Creamy white walls and pure white trim give a small room breathing space and allow furniture to take center stage.

298

Antique game boards are used as decorations and echo the subtle checkerboard pattern in the rug.

299

A large stone hearth is accented with a slab of natural stone as a mantelpiece and is finished with dentil trim.

300

In a twist on tradition, the window rim and sills are rough-hewn while the walls receive the detail. Guitars are hung as art, and blankets are piled on the floor as cushions for game time.

301

Update your decor without completely redecorating by rotating your favorite artwork or photographs. Mix things up to see how different arrangements appeal to you.

302

Maximizing light and cheeriness is the objective of this room, where white walls shine and natural light bounces off the floral chintzes and antiques.

303

There can be many variations of white-on-white. In this room, a vintage basket filled with white chrysanthemums used as a planter is an instant brightener to a monochromatic room.

304

Keeping extra pillows handy without cluttering up a room can be tricky. This pale blue footstool solves the problem simply and elegantly.

Chapter 7 Bedrooms

305

A sepia and rose–colored palette imbues this room with softness and romance. The old photographs leaning on shelves hung above the bed cultivate a sense of history.

306

Fabrics like the slipcover on this chair can be aged by soaking and agitating them in a special "tan" dye in the washing machine.

307

Mixing antique and contemporary furnishings in a peaceful color scheme helps guestrooms appeal to those who may not like a particularly feminine or overly stylized touch.

308

Trunks have lots of storage potential when divided with lift-out trays that are packed efficiently. They can be left open for a decorative touch to display; or they can be stored in a closet or under a bed.

309

The white sails and soft blue
skies in this pair of naval prints
balance the white lamp and bowl
of baby's breath for a striking
composition in the bedroom of
a seaside cottage.

310

Give an otherwise plain bedroom
a twist with a distinctive feature
like antique wall sconces that
instantly add distinction and
drama to the room.

311

Awaken refreshed and retire happy in a bedroom that sings of light and sunshine and a perpetually flowering garden.

312

Look for baskets that already mirror a theme (in this case, flowers), or paint them white and decorate them yourself. Then use them to store pillows and blankets.

313

A decorative window frame made into a mirror captures light, opening up a dark corner space.

314

Guest rooms are great places to indulge in a bit of decorative whimsy—as long as the overall effect is soothing. Wallpaper with lilies of the valley is a nice complement to shades of white, green, and blue throughout the rest of the room.

315

A wicker table is fanciful yet versatile, and can give a guest bedroom a gardenlike feel—especially when topped with a vase overflowing with fresh flowers.

316

Upholstered headboards are
nice for guests to prop pillows
against for reading in full comfort,
and add softness and comfort to
the room.

317

Ribbed cotton chenille bedspreads
and shams are soft and soothing
for summer, and provide a restful
night's sleep.

318

An airy, restful master bedroom is accomplished by keeping things clean and simple with a white-on-white scheme complemented by deep earth tones and natural themes.

319

Arrange a round mirror with a pair of inexpensive white vases for a sleek, modern, and minimalist look in a bedroom.

320

Dried sea urchin shells—with
their distinctive color, shape, and
texture—form attractive and cool
arrangements in simple white
pottery bowls.

321

A built-in bed maximizes the space in a small guest bedroom, while colorful linens make the room inviting and a wall lamp allows guests to read before sleeping.

322

Mix stripes, florals, and solids in
the same color family to get an
eclectic but harmonious, vintage-
inspired look without the vintage
price tag.

323

Feelings of intimacy and repose are brought out by warm colors, such as those found in the drapes, walls, and bedspread of this master bedroom.

324

The blush-colored upholstery is picked up in the room's two side chairs.

325

A simple yet elegant floral arrangement is a quick way to energize a guest bedroom. A predominance of white and green creates a light and fresh feeling.

326

Fashion a unique and colorful bedskirt from a mismatched collection of floral handkerchiefs sewn onto a flat bedsheet and accented with "cotton ball" fringe.

327

A white lace bed skirt adds a soft, romantic touch to this bed that is otherwise bursting with color with its linens, piles of pillows, and duvet cover.

328

Add dimension and character to a dressing table. Giving a lampshade the power of a mini tableaux can make a dresser top really stand out.

329

To give a vintage look to new fabric prints before making them into pillows, tea-dye them or leave them in the sun for a bit. Then use old French linen dish towels as backs.

330

A tonal palette of light pink and brown allows for a range of classic additions, like shells or lamps, that together create a sense of harmony and balance.

331

An antique, handpainted foldaway
kitchen table makes an excellent,
and charming, nightstand/desk
combination perfect for a small
guest room.

332

Two or three dominant colors in a room are all you need to create an eclectic mix without giving an overly busy appearance. The colors can be used in a variety of patterns, however—florals, stripes, and plaids, for instance, are all used here.

333

For an unconventional—yet charming—look, use a dining chair as a bedside table, topped with books and a reading lamp.

334

A floral area rug does wonders to anchor a room's layout and to provide visual interest to a room that features solid colors and very few patterns.

335

Keep plenty of soft blankets and quilts on hand for guests on chilly nights. Easily identify items in a linen closet by affixing handsome metal brackets and handwritten labels to each shelf.

336

This master bedroom's restful effect comes from soft green walls and a white-painted floor. A faux-lamb's-wool rug provides a plush, warm place for bare feet last thing at night and first thing in the morning.

337

A bed you want to sink into is calming and inviting, made so by the soothing neutral color scheme here that's broken up only by the ticking in the bedspread and a delicate floral-patterned blanket.

338

A small tray filled with shells is a lovely stage for a couple of white candles and will be the perfect welcome for guests after a long journey.

339

Add contrast to a two-story master bedroom by creating the illusion of a chair rail: divide a room with paint—a color on the bottom and white on top.

340

This small youth's chair—an antique found at a flea market—is the perfect perch for a big teddy bear and his precious little buddy—and the American flag for a dash of patriotism.

341

If closet space is tight, a ladder provides the hangers guests may need during their temporary stay in a guest room, and keeps everything easily within reach.

342

An armchair and a wall lamp provide a cozy spot for reading or relaxing by the fire, with plenty of books within reach on the shelves behind the chair.

343

A desk can be a welcome and practical addition to a master bedroom as a place to do serious work, write letters, sketch, or contemplate.

344

A great seasonal makeover for any small room is to change the color of one of the walls with a new shade of paint that can capture the feeling of that time of year.

345

Geometrics work with other geometrics as long as one pattern is dominant and all are within the overall color scheme, as with the plaid chair and checkered carpet here.

346

An upholstered paneled screen extends the concept of a headboard, creates a sense of coziness around the bed, and makes a long room more intimate.

347

A clear apothecary jar becomes a nice display vessel for a collection of antique eyeglasses on a dresser top or nightstand.

348

Paneling that's been painted a dark blue enriches a room with cherrywood beds and trim, and helps the crisp matching quilts really stand out.

349

A guest bedroom is the perfect place to showcase a collection of antique trunks found in vintage shops or flea markets. They're perfect for storing extra pillows and blankets.

350

A floral-motif chandelier adorns
a corner stenciled with water
lilies and irises, and bathes the
room in a romantic glow.

351

The drapes in this bedroom
are a set of mix-and-match florals
in colors that complement the
rest of the room.

352

Pockets have been sewn into the sheer half-curtains to hold treasures from the garden.

353

Different floral linens were sewn together to create a unique bedspread.

354

An old barn door nailed to the wall makes a unique country-chic headboard that ties together the barn motif in the eclectic art and accessories.

355

To maintain a sense of serenity while adding a seasonal touch, consider wrapping presents in similarly themed and colored papers that match the room where they will be opened.

356

To create a simple yet rich look in a guest bedroom, decorate with a palette of only two colors. Here, dark blue and white make a dramatic combination.

357

Help a dark room feel warm and inviting by going with a cool, neutral wall color rather than trying to brighten the space. Think subtle and soft and comforting.

358

A weathered cupboard is the perfect repository for a collection of tweed, leather, fine fabrics, and even a small wooden barn model.

359

An armoire doesn't have to be closed. Leave it open and let it speak to your personal style, reflected in your arrangement of the contents.

360

Standing lamps provide light for readers without requiring space for a table. Different heights accommodate the preferences of the bed's occupants.

361

An antique stool is a handy bookstand that can support one or several titles and keep nighttime reading material easy to reach.

362

When a bed is as unique as this Louis XV piece—which still has the handles that were used to move it toward a fire or an open window more than 250 years ago—the best way to dress it is with something simple like a scalloped-edge blanket.

363

White satin and white cotton meet in the white chiffon spread covering this decadently soft and welcoming guest bed.

364

For an all-out romantic look, pile on silk pillows and complete the look with pink sheer emblazoned with gold stars and a plush shag rug underfoot.

365

Boldly patterned wall coverings can dramatize a room's already striking and unique features, like an arched door, high window, or cathedral ceiling.

366

When you're short on closet space, finding attractive places to hang things becomes a challenge. Look for decorative shelves and wall hooks that give you enough room to allow items to fall well away from the wall.

367

Mixing and matching prints isn't a no-no when they're organized around a theme or color scheme, like these striped, plaid, solid, and patterned pillows and linens— all in red, white, blue, and gold.

368

To make a small room with lots of different floral prints appear more expansive, a giant antique mirror is used as a headboard, reflecting light from the windows and creating the illusion of more space.

369

Transform an inexpensive lamp with silk flowers applied with a glue gun. Finish the look by affixing a fanciful ribbon along the bottom edge of the shade.

370

A rail of hooks above a bed makes a unique way to hang artwork. The rose theme of the paintings is carried over to the bouquet on the side table.

371

Transitioning from a bright color like the yellow of this hallway into a soft color like the pale blue of this bedroom sets a relaxing mood for retiring.

372

This bedroom's sense of vitality comes from the many ways flowers and plants are woven into its design: the curtains, the pillow shams, the prints on the side table, and, of course, the pot of daisies.

373

Dried lamb's ear in a white pot complements a simple cupboard painted the palest shade of green but with a white top.

374

Sheer bedcover fabric can be
fashioned over plain pillows and
decorated with fanciful hooks,
buttons, fabric flowers, and
even photos.

375

Create a private space for yourself by transforming a nook in a bedroom. This space gets some of its definition from the striped shade and matching chair fabric.

376

To customize and give formality and elegance to an otherwise plain wood finish, look for pieces like these column toppers that can be glued into place.

377

Note that the wall at the bottom and back of the space under the desk is painted a different color than the upper part of the wall. This provides visual separation.

378

Allow yourself the luxury of
something really striking, even if
you just move it around in your
room for variety. A fine silk throw
in pale colors is the luxurious
item here.

379

Mix and match accessories at will, but be careful to stay within a complementary palette to avoid a cluttered look that clashes.

380

A guest room's dramatically dark carved oak beds are enlivened with colorful pillows made of vintage floral fabrics. An ornate lamp with a floral, fringed shade complements the intricacy of the beds.

381

A round mirror over a simple bedside table can give a feeling of harmony and coziness, and offers guests a means of checking their appearance in the privacy of their room.

382

Heavy curtains on a canopied bed bring drama and authenticity to a bedroom decorated in a style similar to the late 1700s. Curtains originally served to keep out drafts and preserve warmth.

383

A collection of antiques in a palette of subdued reds, grays, and blues gives period quality to this corner of a bedroom. Fresh flowers introduce the present to the past.

384

Wallpapers can be used to cover storage containers, trash bins, even peg rails, and can be an inexpensive way to give a bedroom instant character and charm.

385

Ottomans need not always be accompanied by chairs. Here is one that can be used for a stool or a handy place to toss clothes or throws.

386

Romance doesn't have to be soft and demure. Heat it up with red floors and hot-colored pillowcases and bedspreads.

387

Transform a new wooden dresser by giving it an aged patina look and crystal knobs, lending it an old-fashioned, classy look.

Chapter 8   Kids' Rooms

388

Even a young girl will love the
assortment of prints and patterns
put together here—it's simple,
soothing, and something that can
be grown into.

389

Fashion an easy art center where kids can enjoy "drawing on the walls" by painting a bottom panel of a door with several coats of blackboard paint.

390

The tone of this room is cool, with basic blue walls and crisp white trim. It can change as the child whose room this is grows.

391

A bedspread can establish or support a theme, and can also be easily changed. In this room, the theme is surfing.

392

Kids can be rough on rooms, so you can bring in no-worry furniture that looks good by finding "distressed" pieces like this bookcase, or wear-proof pieces like the rolltop desk and bench.

393

A large globe is an endless source of fascination and learning for kids of all ages. Place it on a desk or nightstand where it will get lots of use.

394

For organizing those first pairs of shoes, try using decorative ceramic, plastic, or leather trays that can be displayed for easy access or stowed away under a bed or in a closet.

395

Victorian pressed-glass curtain tiebacks are as cheerful today as they were more than 100 years ago, and will certainly make little girls happy.

396

Consider your child's current tastes and allow for room to grow by using favorite colors and accenting with collections of personal items that can be replaced or added to over the years.

397

Rooms can be made to feel larger than they really are by using patterns consistently. The checked pattern here is repeated in the draperies, walls, and area rug; florals are repeated on the quilt, pillow, and artwork.

398

Daybeds can double as sofas when friends visit. Baskets can be stored under the bed to hide clutter.

399

Matching upholstered sleigh beds are made for crib-sized mattresses; when the beds are outgrown, they can still be used as daybeds or benches at the end of full-sized beds.

400

When setting up your child's
workspace, think basic and light,
and use stackable boxes and a
bulletin board to help keep clutter
under control.

401

For a cozy feel, striped fabric panels were added to the head- and footboards of this antique bed tucked in the corner of a small child's room.

Chapter 9 Home Offices

402

Create a keepsake of summer seashore collectibles by mounting shells and sea glass inside a frame and hanging it over your desk to remind yourself of the sand and sea air.

403

A collection of glass jars provides a looking glass into a world of white buttons of different shapes and sizes, and creates a unique, interesting accent in a sewing room.

404

Sterling silver is very versatile. It can be used in many ways and always looks great. Here, a toast rack does duty as a mail sorter.

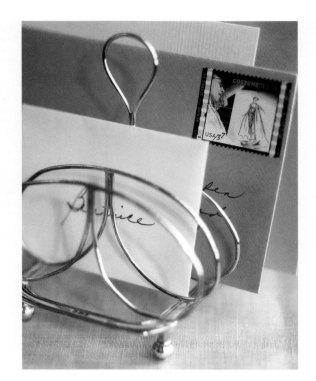

405

The desk is usually the focal point of a home office and needs to be treated as such. If yours is wood, select office accessories that warm up the earth tones.

406

A great clutter-buster is a bulletin board, which can also become an inspiration board for you when filled with favorite photos, postcards, or decorating swatches.

407

Stackable and portable are qualities to be desired in desk accessories. Old wooden drawers and leather in-boxes work for this office.

408

Convert an alcove space into a home office by dividing the space with a drapery panel and painting the office space a contrasting color.

409

A converted closet just large enough for a desk and chair makes a handy home office that can be concealed with decorative curtains.

410

Decorative hardware for doors and cabinets is "jewelry for the home." Incorporating it into a door for a home office can make that utilitarian space more attractive.

411

You may want to try something unique in your private office space. A stencil in an expressive pattern can be just the thing to wake up the wall in front of you. A word to the wise: Practice on paper first!

412

Create a faux bookcase on the door to your office by applying narrow "shelves" to the surface of the door, then sawing off the spines of out-of-date reference books and gluing them above the shelves. Plan the shelves ahead of time so you can accommodate books of a variety of heights.

413

Warm up an off-white foldaway drawer desk with pink accents and fresh flowers for inspiration. A floral seat cushion adds comfort and style to the desk chair.

414

Any room can be made into a home office. Here, a wicker desk has been added to a sunroom to create a bright, cheerful workspace.

415

Recycle a pretty gift box or vintage boxes and fill it with letters, postcards, photos, and special mementos to remind you of many wonderful things at once.

416

Keeping ribbons in sight means they have a better chance of being used. Find interesting clear jars in which to display them and keep them where you'll feel inspired.

417

Centuries-old character comes from paneled wainscoting, half shutters that help conceal the contemporary size and style of the windows, and paint sponged on the walls.

418

Add visual interest to a study with a tall bookshelf made to look like a ladder. It's also the perfect place to display other collectibles.

Chapter 10 Small Rooms

419

If you're inspired by the delicate colors of spring's first blooms, bring the greens and pinks inside. A green wall can serve as a backdrop for floral prints and other collectibles in various shades of pink.

420

Color adds excitement and personality to small rooms—these citrusy stripes of paint and bouquet of fresh tulips punch up the energy of this space.

421

To make the most of a small space, think balance and simplicity of form—as in the matching love seats—and of color—with a neutral palette.

422

Create a nifty nook practically anywhere by defining the space with one eye-catching object. In this space, it's an iron chair softened with a floral pillow and dressed up with antique lace and a silver tea set. And don't forget fresh flowers.

423

Transform a plain lamp into something quirky with buttons. Using plain or patterned buttons and a strong adhesive, begin affixing them around the top of the lampshade and work your way down to the bottom.

424

This area is stylish yet remains comfortable by combining simplicity with comfort, eclectic with classic. The unfinished wooden chest pairs nicely with the unfinished wicker chair; the mix of fabrics complements and contrasts; the silver candelabrum, crystal bowl, and wrought-iron plant stand add classic elements; the angel and the hanging oar bring in personality and whimsy.

425

The soft shades of pink, blue, and green in the ceramics on display are picked up in the different floral pillow fabrics that both contrast and complement each other.

426

Covering a small wall with squares of wallpaper can bring the art of collage to a whole new creative level. Plan the design first by pinning up the squares, then draw chalk outlines on the wall and begin affixing the squares from the center outward.

427

An unframed abstract painting provides a dash of color against the brick wall, further supported here by colorful chairs beside a warm wooden drop-leaf table.

428

Keep a breakfast nook informal with wooden folding chairs that can be painted to complement or contrast with the surroundings. Their simple design allows other elements to take center stage, such as bright colors on doors and a large painting.

429

Create a private Eden by positioning plants of different sizes and types around a bank of sunny windows. Interspersing statuary adds further refinement.

430

The bright color of the yellow wing chair is the focal point of a garden sanctuary and makes the room much more alive.

431

A flower room with a large sink and plenty of storage space can also serve as a handy out-of-the-way wet bar during gatherings.

432

Use an assortment of handled wicker baskets to store shears, planters, and other gardening supplies in a flower room.

433

A stainless steel–topped island
separates a working kitchen
from a casual playroom/den
where the furnishings are practical
and comfortable.

434

Sliding glass doors between two rooms provide additional quiet and create a more distinct space while still allowing light to flow from one room to another.

435

To offset bold fabrics like velvet and chenille, use natural elements that provide texture. In this room, these include a shelled mirror and a raffia floor pillow.

436

If you want "cozy elegance" in a room, include linen in your mix of fabrics. A faded finish and traditional pattern lend a sense of heritage.

437

A large drum-shaped lampshade covered with textured silk has a rich appearance both on and off. When lit, it casts a flattering glow on the room.

438

For a shot of nostalgia and old-fashioned fun, introduce a chiffon throw that's reminiscent of the lacy gowns and lingerie of the 1920s.

439

A white-on-white palette unifies a mix of old and new as a Victorian crib repurposed as a settee pairs with a painted coffee table and an assortment of knick-knacks.

440

An intimate dining nook is created by positioning a small table under a crystal chandelier and opening up the space with a tall, narrow mirror hung on the wall.

441

Make old windows new again by
fashioning them into wall decor,
as with this tall, gothic-style frame
hung over an antique daybed.

442

It takes discipline to keep from filling up a space, but the result of keeping it simple can mean tremendous tranquillity, as in this attic furnished with a hammock for solitary relaxation.

443

A simple stenciled border along the walls, just below the ceiling, picks up the palette and tone of the country mural on the wall by the staircase.

444

The rich earth tones of an eclectic pottery collection help bring the display together and create a sense of unity in the small nook.

445

For comfort and to soften the appearance of this primitive bench, a seat cushion with a hand-sewn cover is added, maintaining the rustic look of the piece.

446

Nooks like this closet converted to a butler's pantry make great spaces for displaying colorful collections, for storing cookies and other treats, and for hiding some kitchen appliances.

447

A linen slipcover, pillow, and half-curtains enhance the country ambience of a room otherwise dominated by wooden furniture.

448

If you crave a place in your home where you can feel calm, resolve to make one. Here, a small space is furnished simply with a welcoming pair of matching wing chairs.

449

Their individuality, fragility, and lovely patterning make these quail eggs worthy of a special spot. They are displayed in a nest of hay in a white enamel vase.

Chapter 11 Laundry Rooms

450

Accessibility maximizes efficiency, which is why laundry and work rooms in particular benefit from long, open shelves, where often-used items can be stored neatly and within reach.

451

Conceal an open under-the-sink or under-counter area—a natural spot for storing unsightly cleaners—with simple curtains hung on a securely fitted rod.

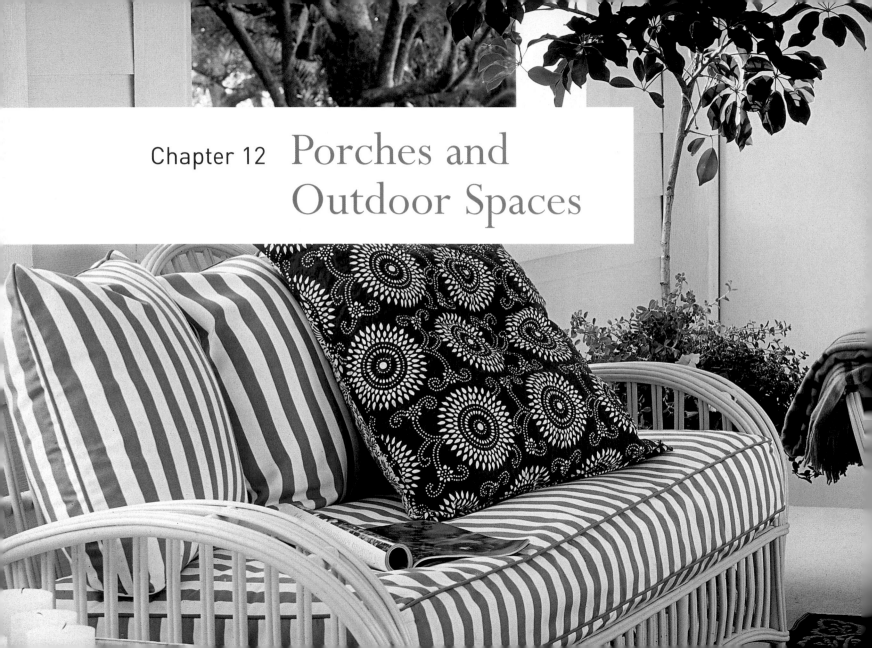

Chapter 12   Porches and Outdoor Spaces

452

Hammocks don't have to go between trees. They can be secured to porch railings, where the addition of a blanket and pillow will make it the most sought-after spot in summer.

453

Brighten up a patio with colorful rugs, pillows, flowers, dining chairs, and even curtains fashioned from fabrics designed to withstand the effects of the sun and rain.

454

Assess the unique nature of a plant to find the pot that's right for it. A low-growing plant is handsome in a stately urn; modulated leaves look nice in a plain container.

455

Floral porcelain teacups perched on old balustrades are used as charming bumblebee drinking stations in a lush garden.

456

Window boxes cleaned of summer's flowers make great receptacles for fall's festive bounty, like colorful pumpkins and gourds.

457

Why not bring the inside out? If you know it's going to be a nice day, put away the plastic patio chairs and treat yourself with some fine furniture.

458

Make a grand porch cozy by creating small seating areas—with loveseat and chairs and also an eating table. Add plenty of pillows to make it inviting and comfortable.

459

Overstuffed pillows on wicker chairs invite rejuvenating breaks on the porch—perhaps even an afternoon nap—with a peaceful view of a garden or the woods.

460

Bold stripes add color and distinction on the floor of a sunporch. When considering paints and styles, choose a paint that's designed to stand up to heavy foot traffic and the effects of the elements.

461

In that wonderful transitional time between spring and summer, make an occasion out of a meal by moving your dining room table outside and using less casual chairs gathered from other rooms.

462

Cobalt and white striped fabric on porch furniture brings the cool blueness of the sky right to the house and creates a peacefulness that promotes relaxation.

Chapter 13 Seasonal Decorating

463

No Memorial Day or Fourth of July celebration is complete without flags. A grouping of flags of different sizes placed in an umbrella stand is at the ready for anyone who gets the urge to wave one.

464

A couple of classic benches and a solid wooden table all painted crisp white become a "picnic table" that stands up to informal and formal meals.

465

Transform a shed into a festive
eating area to celebrate fall.
A gourd-festooned centerpiece
and seating places adorned with
chinaberries are eye-catching
against a plain table and chairs.

466

Vintage greeting cards and dried flower bouquets secured to chairs with twine combine color, texture, history, nature, and a simple greeting all in one decorative accent.

467

Atop a mantle, pair vintage ornaments with other antique display pieces, like this hand-painted ball ornament resting on a McCoy cornucopia vase.

468

Miniature Christmas trees (live or fake) make a beautiful mantel display. For a special family project, assign each member of the family one to decorate, then group them together.

469

Combining treasures is a
wonderful way to bring magic
and meaning to your holiday
decorations. Here, a vintage
transferware compote dish
becomes a home for a lovingly
worn teddy bear holding a
prized bauble.

470

For the myriad occasions when a simple gift is called for, cookies and treats stashed into decorative tins are the perfect thing. Packed properly, the food will stay fresh for several days. The containers make festive decorations—and easily accessible gifts—for the kitchen or dining room.

471

Infusing a Christmas tree with ornaments of every color calls for other decorations to be more refined, like garlands of pine boughs and gifts wrapped in earth tones of gold, green, and rich brown.

472

Get creative with organizers, especially for holiday items. Here, a vintage egg carton now makes an excellent storage unit for ornaments that need to be handled with care.

473

Cardboard coasters and plain paper goods become novel gift tags by simply lacing a beautiful ribbon through a hole and attaching them to packages.

474

Green and gold are elegant color choices for the holidays, and they get a new twist when the greens are muted and aqua-hued, and the gold is more yellow. If you don't have a fireplace, you can still hang stockings from a banister or, as here, from a piano.

475

The holidays are the perfect occasion to decorate with themed collectibles, like the vintage Santas displayed on this mantel and table.

476

Turn plain manila tags into personalized Christmas tree ornaments by gluing them on vintage holiday cards and decorating with glitter.

477

Add a festive touch to your front door—or any door in your house—by hanging a collection of small bells that will add merriment to the season every time the door is opened or closed.

478

Early-American Christmas trees were decorated with paper chains, strings of cranberries, dried quinces, painted walnuts, feathers, and cookies for children.

479

Wreaths fashioned from fresh
evergreen boughs are both
fragrant and elegant. They can be
accessorized in many ways. This
one has nature in its theme,
incorporating dried flowers,
milkweed pods, pinecones,
and a feather.

480

Amaryllises wreathed in pinecones and boxwood make a stunning seasonal centerpiece for a dinner table, entry table, or coffee table.

481

A white corner cupboard is an excellent display case for seasonal items in the traditional Christmas colors of red and green in all their variations.

482

Now's the time to bring out any fun or funky boxes you found at flea markets throughout the year so that they can be used as gift boxes. Ribbons and ornaments make them extra special.

483

To turn your cards into a nifty decoration. Center a piece of narrow ribbon over a wider one and sew at the top to secure. Using holding clips from an office-supply store, sew them onto the ribbon, leaving enough space in between for cards. Next, glue buttons over the stitching.

484

Brightly patterned seasonal tablecloths can be sewn into beautiful stockings, which are especially meaningful when they're personalized with someone's initials.

485

Festive poinsettia glasses on a two-tiered vintage pie stand add the perfect touch to your seasonal decorating.

486

Special take-home holiday goody bags are simple to create and beautiful outside and in. Stack cookies in a baking cup, trim the cup with ribbon, put the cup in a cellophane bag, trim the bag with zigzagged pinking shears, and secure with a ribbon. You can also include the recipe and a personalized gift tag.

487

Working with nontraditional holiday colors, such as lilac, plum, and silver—this homeowner's favorite colors—creates a romantic holiday atmosphere.

488

A long mantel is home to cream-colored pillar candles of all shapes and sizes, which complement the lights on the tree and add an extra-warm glow to the room.

489

Simple festive touches are sometimes all that's needed to bring the holidays home. Here, miniature spruce trees are grouped and surrounded by red pears. Red pillar candles accent the centerpiece.

490

Create a welcoming holiday arrangement composed of candles wrapped in seasonal papers, with bows, sprigs of holly, and Christmas tree ornaments.

491

A cozy cottage's white theme makes for an almost anything-goes setting for the holidays. An all-natural tree evokes Christmases past and fills the room with the scent of fresh pine.

492

To give a bedroom a festive touch, a string of red glass beads is laced through a bed frame and accented with wreaths of paperwhites.

493

Stray from the expected by introducing a nontraditional color into the holiday scheme. Here, teal-blue balls and tree skirt add a modern touch to gold stars and ribbon.

494

Antique needlework and blooming agapanthus show off holiday postcards from the early 20th century, supported in old frogs (ornamental flower holders).

495

Vintage letters bring Old World character to this traditional red, green, gold, and silver tree, and a small ladder next to the tree provides a lovely perch for small gifts.

496

The new take on an old Christmas tradition is easy to make: this Advent calendar is fashioned from flash cards, paper clips, and ribbon, with tiny ornaments as treats.

497

An enclosed wraparound porch is a favorite spot for seasonal decorating. Here, synthetic green trees with simple white lights complement the already established black-and-white theme.

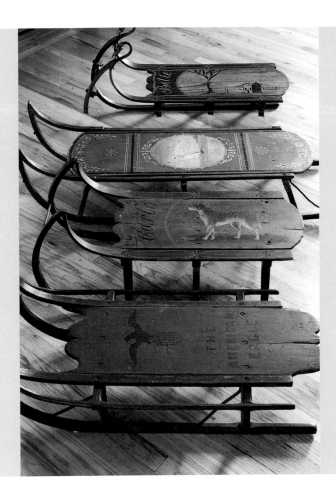

498

Antique sleds make wonderful wintertime display pieces, to be admired on their own or piled high with gifts.

499

A small tinsel tree with a glittering gold star is the perfect topping for a small coffee table and is a modern foil to the big, traditional tree in the back of the room.

500

Go for an 18th-century country look by making a pineapple—the classic symbol of hospitality—the centerpiece of a decorative mantel.

Photo Credits

Index